PRAISE FOR

The Win-Win Negotiator

"A BULL'S-EYE HIT IN THE CENTER OF COMMUNICA-
TION AND TRANSACTION EXCELLENCE."

—Dr. Denis Waitley,
author of *The Double Win* and
The Joy of Working

"GUIDES PEOPLE THROUGH THE NEGOTIATING PRO-
CESS. . . . Will serve your negotiating needs, whether they are
with your boss, your customers, spouse, or child. USE IT TO
EVERYBODY'S ADVANTAGE."

—*The Phoenix Gazette*

"*THE WIN-WIN NEGOTIATOR* IS A WIN-WIN FOR YOU—
BETTER BUSINESS AND BETTER RELATIONSHIPS. . . .
THE SOONER YOU READ THE BOOK, THE BETTER OFF
YOU WILL BE."

—Hendrie Weisinger, Ph.D.,
author of *Nobody's Perfect* and
The Critical Edge

"Underscore[s] the foundation of the *successful* deals we have
put together over the years."

—Theodore J. Wolfe,
Executive Vice-President, Welch Foods

"Captures the essence of the successful negotiation process . . .
Written in a very easy-to-read, enjoyable format."

—Ted Fowler,
President, Golden Corral Corporation

"FINALLY, AN EASY-TO-READ, COMPREHENSIBLE
BOOK ON HUMAN AND PRODUCTIVE NEGOTIATIONS.
THANK YOU, DRS. RECK AND LONG, FOR SHOWING US
THAT PEOPLE, THE HUMAN RESOURCE, ARE OUR
GREATEST ASSETS IN NEGOTIATIONS AND LIFE."

—Charles A. Garfield, Ph.D.,
author of *Peak Performance*

The WIN-WIN Negotiator

HOW TO NEGOTIATE
FAVORABLE AGREEMENTS THAT LAST

Ross R. Reck, Ph.D., and Brian G. Long, Ph.D.

POCKET BOOKS

New York   London   Toronto   Sydney   Tokyo   Singapore

POCKET BOOKS, a division of Simon & Schuster Inc.
1230 Avenue of the Americas, New York, NY 10020

Copyright © 1985, 1987 by Brian G. Long and Ross R. Reck

Published by arrangement with the authors
Library of Congress Catalog Card Number: 87-61727

ISBN: 0-671-67698-9

First Pocket Books trade paperback printing August 1989

10 9 8 7 6 5 4 3

POCKET and colophon are trademarks of Simon & Schuster Inc.

Printed in the U.S.A.

WIN WIN WIN *The Symbol*

The Win-Win Negotiator's symbol is intended to remind us that, while we would all like to win at our professional and private lives, it is impossible for us to continually do so unless we are willing to help others win with us.

Acknowledgments

W̲E recognize that, without the help of others, this book would not have been possible. We wish to offer our highest praise:

To *Ms. Heidi Hougham* and *Ms. Kaye Settle,* who suggested that we write the book in the first place. Without their encouragement, this book would have never been written.

To *Kelsey Tyson,* for his inspiration, encouragement, and guidance.

To *Ms. Beth Bradfish,* whose skillful editing polished our rough edges, and *Darlene Gerster,* for introducing her to us.

To *Ms. Jean Cox,* for crossing our "T's" and dotting our "I's," and polishing our punctuation and grammar.

To *Maril Adrian* and *Harry Paul* for all their many efforts in getting this project off the ground.

To *Karen Abbott,* for guiding our efforts and lighting our path.

To all the people at Blanchard Training and Development for their friendship.

To *Marcia, Katie,* and *Philip Reck,* and to *Marie Long,* the members of our families who commented on our rough drafts and encouraged us while we wrote and rewrote the manuscript.

To *Roger Fisher* and *William Ury* for their efforts in developing the concept of *principled negotiation.*

To *Jim Woodson,* for stimulating our thinking and broadening our prospective.

To many friends and seminar participants over the years who kindly reviewed our manuscript.

THE WIN-WIN NEGOTIATOR

Foreword

When Spencer Johnson and I began to write THE ONE MINUTE MANAGER, we decided to put it in the form of a parable for two reasons. First of all, Spencer had a lot of experience writing parables from putting together his ValuTales Series for children, and I taught and trained in parables. Secondly, when we thought of the most powerful things we had ever read in our lives, most of them happened to be parables. For example, the parables of the Bible were always one of the most powerful parts of the Scriptures to me. JONATHAN LIVINGSTON SEAGULL was a marvelous little book, and one I just loved as a child was THE LITTLE PRINCE. Og Mandino's series of the greatest salesmen of them all were charming and informative. For these reasons we decided to write a parable.

Little did I know that teaching management by parable would be such a tremendous hit among managers in all kinds of organizations, but since it was, I have decided to contiue to present the best, most useful management concepts to managers through the use of parables. When Ross Reck and Brian Long sent me a copy of THE WIN-WIN NEGOTIATOR, I was thrilled about it. While some people might question my enthusiasm because it is too familiar in format to THE ONE MINUTE MANAGER, I have no problem with that. In fact, that's why I like THE WIN-WIN NEGOTIATOR. It's written in the form of a parable in a clear, easy to understand way that should help everyone in all kinds of relationships, move toward a win-win situation. The four basic steps to becoming a Win-Win Negotiator are: *establishing win-win plans, developing win-win relationships, forming win-win agreements,* and *performing win-win maintenance.* These steps are simple, but powerful ways of increasing human satisfaction and performance.

I recommend THE WIN-WIN NEGOTIATOR without reservation. I think you will find it helpful and another step down the road to taking potentially complicated management concepts and making them simple and useable for managers in every kind of organization.

Kenneth Blanchard, Ph.D.
Co-author, THE ONE MINUTE MANAGER

Introduction

In this brief book, we present the Win-Win method of negotiating. It represents a distillation of what we have learned from our studies in management and the behavioral sciences concerning how to successfully deal with other people. The result is a simple, straight-forward and easy-to-use method of negotiating which helps you achieve the agreement you want, and at the same time, assures that the person you're dealing with feels good about you, the agreement and himself as well. Thus, both parties win and are therefore committed to holding up their end of the agreement.

We have found this method of negotiating to be useful in virtually all types of negotiations whether it be between labor and management, husband and wife, buyer and seller, or parent and child.

We hope you enjoy reading *The Win-Win Negotiator*. Furthermore, we hope you apply and use what you learn from this book and that doing so makes a difference in the success and happiness in your life and in the lives of those with whom you negotiate.

— Ross R. Reck, Ph.D.
— Brian G. Long, Ph.D.

Contents

ONCE there was a bright young man who was searching for the secret to success.

His goal was simple: He wanted to be successful in both his professional and private lives.

The young man's search took him to many different parts of the world.

He visited extensively with many successful company presidents, board chairmen, managers, inventors, authors, politicians, movie stars, and television personalities. He took careful notes of what each of these very successful people told him.

These visits taught him many things. He learned that a businessman could not be successful if he couldn't convince other people to buy his product or service. A manager could not be successful unless he could convince his subordinates to enthusiastically carry out his decisions. Likewise, a politician could not be successful unless he could convince other people to accept his point of view.

The more people the young man visited and the more he thought about all that he had seen and heard, the more clearly the message came into focus.

"It's painfully simple," the young man finally concluded. "The secret to success is being able to effectively deal with people. This means that the more effectively I can deal with other people, the more successful I can become."

The young man was excited about having discovered the secret to success and was anxious to improve his ability to effectively deal with people. While doing some initial research, he discovered a whole field of knowledge dedicated to effectively dealing with people. This field was called **NEGOTIATION**.

"Excellent!" thought the young man. This should be easier than I thought, since there are dozens of books written about negotiation and I get brochures in the mail all the time for negotiation seminars.

During the next year the young man read several negotiation books and attended a number of seminars. He was fascinated by all that he was taught. He learned about the "hard nosed" style of negotiation and about the "nice guy" or "soft" style. He also learned a number of tactics and tricks which he could use to out-fox his negotiation opponents.

The young man was now more excited than ever. Everything seemed like it was going to be so easy. "Success," he thought, "is just around the corner."

One by one, the young man tried to put the ideas he had learned into practice. Much to his dismay, however, the results he experienced were very disappointing. When he tried the hard-nosed method of negotiating, he discovered that it generated more animosity and resentment from the people he was dealing with than agreement. When he tried the "nice guy" approach, he found hard-nosed negotiators took advantage of him. Finally, he found that using tactics and tricks to out-fox the people he dealt with tended to undermine his credibility rather than resolve problems.

Discouraged, but still convinced that being able to effectively deal with people was the secret to success, the young man pondered his poor performance as a negotiator. "Surely there's got to be a better way," he thought.

That evening, as he was reading the paper, the young man came across a feature story about a man from a nearby city who was acclaimed as the "negotiator's negotiator." The story centered on how this man had successfully negotiated a solution to a seemingly hopeless and sticky problem. The writer of the article was so impressed with this man's record as a successful negotiator that he referred to him as a "master of the game."

"This guy sounds like a sure winner," thought the young man. "I'll bet he's got the world by the tail. I wonder if he might be willing to share some of the secrets of his success with me."

On the next day, to satisfy his curiosity, the young man telephoned the negotiator's secretary. He explained that he had read some fascinating things about her boss's exploits as a negotiator, and wondered if he would be willing to share some of his secrets with him.

"Why, of course!" replied the secretary. "He loves to talk to people about negotiating."

"You really don't think he'll mind?" asked the young man.

"Heavens no," replied the secretary. "In fact, you're the second person this week to call for an interview. When would you like to see him?" asked the secretary. "He's available all week, except Tuesday and Thursday afternoons."

"Is that when he holds his staff meetings?" asked the young man.

"No," chuckled the secretary. "That's when he plays golf."

"Golf!" exclaimed the young man. "He must really be something if he can afford the time to go golfing twice a week."

"That he is," replied the secretary. "He golfs at least twice a week. I think you'll understand why after you talk to him. Now, when would you like your appointment?"

"How about Thursday at 10:00 a.m.?" asked the young man.

"Fine," said the secretary. "We'll look forward to seeing you then."

The young man was both curious and fascinated. He was looking forward to meeting this special person.

W HEN the young man arrived at the negotiator's office, he was warmly greeted by a secretary who seemed very excited about her job.

"Go right in," she said with a smile. "He's been expecting you."

The young man approached the negotiator's office with nervous enthusiasm, curious about what kind of superman he would find on the other side of the door. As he entered the office, he found a slightly-built, balding man gingerly stroking a golf ball into a plastic cup.

"Nice to meet you," said the man in an enthusiastic but soft-spoken voice as he put his putter back into his golf bag.

"I'm sorry to interrupt you," replied the young man.

"Nonsense!" said the man as he motioned for the young man to sit down. "Nothing is more important than people. That's one of the reasons why I play golf. It gives me a chance to interact with people.

"Now, what can I do for you?" asked the man as he settled into a nearby chair.

The young man explained how he had concluded that the secret to success in people's professional or private lives was their ability to effectively negotiate.

"I couldn't agree with you more," the negotiator said with a smile.

The young man went on to explain how he had read several absorbing books and attended numerous seminars, but nothing he learned gave him the results he was looking for.

"That doesn't surprise me," commented the negotiator.

The young man continued, "The other evening I was reading the feature article in the newspaper concerning your success as a negotiator. As a result, I became curious about how you do it. I hope you will consider sharing the secrets of your success with me."

"I'd be delighted," beamed the negotiator.

The young man continued, "I was very impressed with how the reporter who wrote the article referred to you as a 'master of the game.' I want to become a master of the game, too."

"I'd like to have a talk with the reporter who made that statement," said the negotiator in a wary voice. "I know he meant no harm, but that statement told me that he doesn't know much about negotiation."

"What do you mean?" asked the young man.

The negotiator continued, "The first thing you have to realize about negotiating is that it's not a game. The problem with games is that while they produce winners, they also produce losers."

The young man scratched his forehead. He was not totally sure what the negotiator meant.

"Let me explain," said the negotiator. "Do you participate in any sports like golf, tennis, or softball?"

"I play tennis," replied the young man.

"All right then," replied the negotiator. "When you beat somebody at tennis, especially if you really clobber your rival, what incentive do you leave?"

"To get even the next time we play," answered the young man.

"Precisely!" exclaimed the negotiator. "He's out gunning for you, and if you beat this person once too often, he won't want to play with you anymore, will he?"

"You're right there," said the young man. "I lost a good tennis partner that way once."

"Now I ask you," queried the negotiator, "is this the way to run a successful business, or for that matter, a successful life, family, or marriage?"

"I guess not," answered the young man.

The negotiator continued, "Do you gain friends or strengthen relationships with other people by beating them at something and making them feel like losers?"

"No, I guess you don't," answered the young man.

"That's why it's wrong to consider negotiation a game," stated the negotiator. "As I said earlier, the problem with viewing negotiation as a game is that games produce losers and losers have no incentive to help *you* become successful."

The negotiator continued, "It took me a long time, but I finally figured out that successful negotiations do not produce losers, only winners. That's why I call myself a **WIN-WIN NEGOTIATOR.**"

"A Win-Win Negotiator?" asked the young man with a puzzled look on his face. "I've heard of negotiators referred to as winners before, but I don't think I've ever heard of a Win-Win Negotiator."

"I'm not surprised," replied the Win-Win Negotiator, "because society, with its preoccupation with athletic contests, sets us up to applaud winners and look down at losers. When you think of it, we're pretty much conditioned to the idea that every winner has to be offset by at least one loser. The problem with carrying this winner-loser philosophy over into your professional and personal lives is that no one, including yourself, wants to feel like a loser.''

"I see what you mean about no one wanting to feel like a loser, but I'm still not sure what being a Win-Win Negotiator is," said the young man.

"Here, look at this," replied the Win-Win Negotiator as he handed the young man a plaque from his desk. "I keep it in front of me all the time to remind myself what being a Win-Win Negotiator is all about.''

***

*Losers Don't Come
Through For You*

But

Winners Do!

***

"Think about it for a moment," said the Win-Win Negotiator. "When do you feel the most motivated to live up to things you've agreed to?"

"When I feel good about the agreement and what I'm going to get out of it," replied the young man.

"You mean when holding up your end of the agreements makes you feel like a winner?" asked the Win-Win Negotiator with a smile on his face.

"I think I'm beginning to see what you're driving at," said the young man.

"Let me ask you another question," continued the Win-Win Negotiator. "When do you feel *least* motivated to live up to an agreement?"

The young man thought for a moment and then replied, "When I feel I've come out on the short end of the deal — a loser."

"I think you're catching on," beamed the Win-Win Negotiator, "but let me give you a real life example that will illustrate what being a Win-Win Negotiator is all about.

"Several years ago, a professional baseball player was deadlocked on his salary negotiations with a team that had just acquired his services. The player wanted a lot more money than the owner was proposing, for he was certain that his just playing on the team would sell more tickets and therefore generate more profit for the owner. The owner was not convinced. He doubted there would be enough additional fans to offset the increase in salary, especially given that the club had just posted record attendance the past year."

"Let me guess what happened," said the young man.

"Go ahead," replied the Win-Win Negotiator.

"The owner eventually said, 'take it or leave it,' and the player accepted it because it was still a very good salary," answered the young man.

"On the contrary," replied the Win-Win Negotiator. "These people were both Win-Win Negotiators, not win-lose negotiators. So they worked out a two-part agreement which satisfied both parties. First, the ball player agreed to accept a lower salary than he originally asked for, *if* the seasonal attendance was less than that of the previous year. Second, if the coming year's attendance exceeded the previous year's attendance, the player would receive fifty cents for each additional ticket sold over that level."

"I see what you mean now by Win-Win Negotiations," said the young man, "because neither party came out on the short end of the deal."

"Precisely!" shouted the Win-Win Negotiator. "Both parties had a strong incentive to hold up their end of the agreement. The ball player was motivated to work hard to bring more fans into the ball park, and the owner was motivated to pay him for his efforts if he succeeded.''

''Fascinating!'' exclaimed the young man enthusiastically, ''but just out of curiosity, what happened during that next year?''

''Attendance set another new record,'' said the Win-Win Negotiator. ''This netted the ball player more than $200,000 in additional salary and netted the owner far more in additional profits.''

''Your example is convincing,'' said the young man, ''but how is it that you happened to know so much about this particular negotiation?''

''For now, let's just say I know the agent who negotiated the contract very well,'' beamed the Win-Win Negotiator.

''I'll bet you do,'' smiled the young man with a growing sense of admiration for the Win-Win Negotiator.

The young man paused with an inquisitive look on his face. ''From what you've said, I'm convinced that the Win-Win Negotiation concept has merit, but how can I put it to work for myself? Do you have some kind of a manual that I can borrow?''

"You don't need a manual," replied the Win-Win Negotiator. All that you really need to remember are four basic steps. And, rather than giving those to you myself, I'd like you to talk with a few people I've recently negotiated with. I think you'll find it more interesting to learn from a variety of true Win-Win Negotiators."

Now the young man was really puzzled. "You mean that your negotiation opponents are also Win-Win Negotiators?"

"Many of them are," came the reply, "but I don't call them opponents anymore. You don't have opponents in Win-Win Negotiations."

While the look of surprise was still on the young man's face, the Win-Win Negotiator called for his secretary to bring in his appointment calendar for the last several months. He wrote out a list of names, addresses, and telephone numbers.

"Pick out the names of a few people on this list and give them a call. If you tell them who you are and that you want to learn about Win-Win Negotiations, they'll be happy to talk to you. My secretary can help you get started. Also, let's plan to get together next Tuesday morning to discuss what you've learned. You'll have to excuse me now, I have a golf game in 45 minutes."

"Out for a little relaxation?" queried the young man.

"Yes and no," came the reply. "You'll see what I mean between now and next Tuesday...."

THE young man's first appointment turned out to be with a Mr. John Friedman, a successful looking man in his 40s, who said that he was always glad to talk about Win-Win Negotiating.

"The Win-Win Negotiator tells me, that to become a Win-Win Negotiator, all I really have to know is four basic steps," began the young man. "And from what I've already heard, Win-Win Negotiations must have something to do with working toward a mutual agreement rather than with trying to badger the other party into seeing things your way. Is that true?"

"Not a bad thought," replied Friedman. "Working toward mutual agreement is certainly part of the Win-Win concept. But that's not the first step."

After a pause, Friedman continued, "One of my favorite authors was a frustrated mathematician by the name of Lewis Carroll, who among other things, wrote *Alice in Wonderland*. There's an important lesson about goal setting in that book when Alice is talking to the Cheshire Cat:

"Would you tell me, please, which way I ought to go from here?"

"That depends a good deal where you want to go to," said the Cat.

"I don't much care where," said Alice.

"Then it doesn't matter which way you go," said the Cat.

"I think you're saying that the first step in the Win-Win Negotiation process is to do a little advance planning," asserted the young man.

"Exactly," replied Friedman.

Seeming to change the subject, he continued, "Are you going on a vacation this year?"

"Why, yes," replied the young man. "In about two months my family and I are going to a recreation/camping area for about twelve days."

Friedman smiled, "It sounds like you've been doing some planning."

"We sure have. In fact, we've been planning for over six months."

The young man could see that Friedman was driving at something as he probed further by asking,

"Did you ever go on a vacation without a plan?"

"I wouldn't dream of it," declared the young man. "My vacation time is too valuable."

"Plans are important to me, too," Friedman replied. "But it was the Win-Win Negotiator that introduced me to the idea of Win-Win Plans."

"Win-Win Plans?" asked the young man with a puzzled look on his face.

"Yes," responded Friedman. "Establishing Win-Win Plans is the first step and therefore the foundation of the Win-Win Negotiation Process. Believe me, if this step is ignored or improperly done, the chances for a successful negotiation become slim."

"But how does Win-Win Planning differ from any other kind of negotiation planning?" asked the young man.

Friedman continued, "You see, in traditional planning, you first decide what it is you want from the party you're going to negotiate with. This is your negotiation goal. Then you develop a plan that will help you accomplish this goal during the negotiation."

"I don't see anything wrong with this approach," said the young man.

"Most people don't," responded Friedman, "but there is a problem. You see, such plans are often developed without giving enough concern to the fact that the other party has goals that he would also like to accomplish. Thus, if the goals of the other party are not considered during the planning process, how likely is it that the plan will result in a favorable agreement with the other party?"

"Not very," said the young man, "because the other party will have little or nothing to gain from such an agreement."

"Of course not," said Friedman. "Win-Win Planning, on the other hand, does take into account the goals of the other party. The Win-Win Planning process recognizes that people are unlikely to enter into an agreement, much less honor it, if they see themselves as gaining nothing from it. Thus, the essence of establishing Win-Win Plans is to develop ways in which you can help other people accomplish their goals while they, in turn, help you accomplish your goals."

"Is establishing a Win-Win Plan difficult?" asked the young man.

"Actually, it's quite easy," said Friedman. "The Win-Win Planning process begins with deciding, in specifics, the goals you wish to accomplish during the negotiation. This step is critical, because if you're not sure what you want out of the negotiation, it makes no sense to take the planning process any further."

"You're saying," said the young man, "that if you don't know where you're going, it doesn't make any sense trying to figure out how to get there."

"Exactly," responded Friedman. "Now, once you've agreed on your own goals, the next thing you need to do is to try, as well as you can, to anticipate the goals of the party you're going to negotiate with. Remember, just like you, the other party also has goals he wants to achieve during the negotiation. If he didn't have them, he would not be interested in negotiating with you in the first place."

"I can see why this is so important," said the young man. "Since a Win-Win Plan should consider the goals of the other party, it would be impossible to develop such a plan if you didn't have some ideas of what those goals were."

"Right again," said Friedman. "You really catch on fast."

"What's next?" asked the young man.

Friedman continued, "Once you've identified both sets of goals, you then compare them to determine those areas where you and the other party already agree. These areas don't need to be negotiated, only verified during subsequent discussions with the other party. Knowing this is important for two reasons: first, it prevents you from spending valuable time discussing things you already agree on, and second, it provides a common foundation upon which the rest of your Win-Win Plan can be built."

"That makes a lot of sense," said the young man. "But how do you handle those areas where you and the other party are likely to disagree?"

"Good question," answered Friedman. "Once you're aware of those areas of probable agreement, it's time to develop some alternate solutions to reconcile those areas where you'll probably disagree. Here you may need to exercise some creativity and ingenuity in planning how to bring your divergent interests together to form a true Win-Win agreement. This is the most critical and challenging step in the Win-Win Planning process, and I might add, the one that I think is the most fun."

Friedman, seeming to change the subject again, said, "Let's go back and talk about your vacation for a moment. How did you and your family decide on where you're going?"

"Well, my kids wanted to go horseback riding, I wanted to see some new countryside, and my wife just wanted to relax, swim, and get some sun. Limited by this year's budget, each of us expressed what we wanted to do during our vacation. We then listed a number of alternatives and discussed them until we were able to agree on a vacation plan that accomplished all of our goals."

"I'm impressed," replied Friedman. "You already know how to develop a Win-Win Plan."

"I do?"

"You sure do; you just don't recognize it," said Friedman. "You looked at your goals, looked at your family's goals, took into consideration any limiting factors, and then came up with a plan that allowed all family members to get what they wanted. That's a Win-Win Plan if I've ever seen one."

Friedman continued. "Tell me, since you wanted to see scenery, why didn't you plan a vacation like, say, a 2000 mile bus tour?"

"Why, I could never do that. I might think I was going to enjoy myself, but my wife hates busses and my kids would go crazy. Then I would go crazy. It just wouldn't be much of a vacation."

"You're really telling me that since the rest of your family wouldn't accomplish their goals, you really wouldn't accomplish your own goals, either. However, with your Win-Win Plan, I'll bet your entire family will have a good time on your vacation."

"You've convinced me that Win-Win Plans work," said the young man, "but establishing this plan seems like it could be complicated."

"Not really," said Friedman. "Let me give you an example.

"A number of years ago, I wanted to buy my first real home, but I just didn't quite have the income necessary to buy the type of home my wife and I wanted unless I could negotiate a 12% increase in salary with my boss. When I finally got around to approaching him about this, he responded by saying, 'Well, what's your plan?'

"I was very surprised by that question, but I decided to be open with him since he tended to be a fair person. 'The way I see it, I have two possible plans of action,' I answered. 'Plan A would be to take the 'hard-nosed' approach and demand a 12% raise or else. Plan B would be to take the 'nice guy' approach and say that I really would appreciate it if I could get a 12% raise. But I don't really feel good about either one so maybe I should just forget it.'

"At this point, my boss leaned back in his chair and said, 'Not so quickly. Frankly, I'm surprised that neither of your alternatives is a Win-Win Plan.'

"'What do you mean?' I asked.

"'Well,' he said, 'In both of your alternatives, you made it very clear what you want me to do to help you achieve your goal — the 12% raise. However, you made no mention of what you plan to do in return to help me achieve my goals. As such, if I were to give you the raise, you would win but I wouldn't.

Now how motivated does that leave me to give you a raise?' he asked.

"'Not very,' I replied.

"'Of course not!" exclaimed the boss. 'That's why you need to develop a Win-Win Plan. Now let's take a look at my goals. What do you think might be one of my more important ones?' he asked.

"I thought for a moment and said, 'Well, you want our department to be successful so that you, as our manager, can make a good impression on those above you.'

"'Okay,' said the boss. 'Assuming that both you and I agree that we want to continue our current working relationship, what contribution can you make toward this goal that might be worth a 12% raise to me?'

"'Well,' I replied, 'I could offer to take on some of your administrative details so you could spend more of your time managing the department.'

"'Would this be worth a 12% raise to me?' asked the boss.

"'Probably so,' I answered. 'You are continually saying how you hate it and how it keeps you from doing your job. In fact, you've been talking about hiring a new person just to handle some of your administrative details, but this year's budget can't handle another full time person. However, paying me an additional 12% would be far less expensive and it would give you some of the administrative relief you've been looking for.'

"'All right then, how does offering to take some administrative burden from me in exchange for a 12% raise differ from your previous two plans?' asked the boss.

"'Well,' I answered, 'this plan takes into account both of our sets of goals and thus affords both of us the opportunity to win. Furthermore, if the agreement is reached, both of us will be highly motivated to honor our commitments.'

"'Exactly!'' he pronounced. 'This is the essence of a Win-Win Plan — finding a way to reconcile both sets of goals so that both parties win.'''

"Did your Win-Win Plan work?" the young man asked Friedman.

"Indeed it did," answered Friedman. "I got my raise and my boss eventually got promoted. Furthermore, because of my familiarity with the administrative aspects of the job, I eventually became my boss's replacement."

"Your former boss sounds like someone I'd like to meet," said the young man.

"You already have," responded Friedman. "He's the Win-Win Negotiator."

"That's fantastic!" the young man replied. "But what about the other three steps in the Win-Win process?"

"They are just as important," Friedman replied. "But I'm going to let someone else tell you about the next step. Let me see your list of names."

After a few seconds, Friedman spotted a familiar name and helped the young man set up an appointment for the next afternoon.

As the young man left Friedman's office, he took a few moments to record in his notebook the things he had just learned....

Establishing Win-Win Plans is simple. You need only to:

1. Agree on your own goals.
2. Anticipate the goals of the other party.
3. Determine areas of probable agreement.
4. Develop Win-Win solutions to reconcile areas of probable disagreement.

Having discovered the importance of Win-Win Planning to successful negotiation, the young man approached his next appointment with understandable enthusiasm. His next teacher, an employee of a medium sized export-imort company turned out to be Bill Jackson, a tall, impressive man only a few years his senior. Again, he was impressed by the warm greeting and how comfortable he was made to feel in a matter of moments.

He explained about meeting the Win-Win Negotiator, and what he had learned from John Friedman about formulating Win-Win Plans.

"I assume that the next step involves getting down to business," began the young man.

"Not quite," responded Jackson. "Before you get down to business, it's extremely important that you remember who you're getting down to business with."

"What do you mean?" the young man asked with a bewildered look on his face.

Jackson paused for a moment and then continued, "Have you ever been short of money for lunch and had to borrow a few dollars to tide you over?"

"Of course," responded the young man without hesitation.

"When this occurred, did you go up and ask a total stranger if you could borrow the money?" asked Jackson.

"Of course not," came the response. "I wouldn't have the nerve."

"So who did you borrow the money from?" asked Jackson.

"A friend I work with," came the reply.

"Did your friend have you sign an I.O.U. and get it notarized and witnessed?"

"Of course not. He trusts me. Furthermore, I would have been offended if he had even asked."

"That's good, because now you can appreciate the importance of having a relationship with someone you wish to deal with. I think you'll agree that having such relationships with the right people can certainly make negotiating something like a small loan a lot easier. And, just think of the impact that having a good relationship with the person you're negotiating with could have on a large scale negotiation."

"Are you saying that the next step in the Win-Win Negotiation process is to develop relationships with the people you're going to negotiate with?'' asked the young man.

"Yes," answered Jackson. "But not just ordinary relationships. You need to develop Win-Win Relationships. For the same reasons that you would have trouble borrowing money from a total stranger, people in general are reluctant to commit to or enter agreements with people they don't know or trust. If you've ever tried to deal with a total stranger, you've probably noticed his guard was up, his behavior may have been defensive, and he probably tried hard to keep the conversation as non-committal as possible. Indeed, strangers are very difficult people to form Win-Win agreements with. On the other hand, if you were to convert this stranger into someone you knew and who trusted you, you would find him much easier to deal with. You would be far more comfortable with this person's motives and *vice versa*. Furthermore, you both would have a foundation of trust to build upon when you got down to discussing business in earnest. That's why I have this plaque on my desk:''

***

Never Negotiate With Strangers

***

"It serves as a constant reminder of the importance of getting to know people *before* you get down to business with them."

"I agree with what you're saying," said the young man, "but how does a Win-Win Relationship differ from any other relationship?"

"Win-Win Relationships go a step further than, say, the casual relationships you've formed at work," answered Jackson. "You see, Win-Win Relationships are consciously formed with the intent of getting the two parties to feel relaxed, open, and comfortable in dealing with each other. Basically, Win-Win Relationships are formed by the individuals involved, with the intent of bettering each other. As such, they're not only comfortable dealing with each other, they actually look forward to it."

After a thoughtful pause, the young man asked, "You've convinced me of the importance of Win-Win Relationships, but how do I go about developing them?"

"Easy," said Jackson. "You start by planning some activities which will provide the opportunity for a positive relationship to develop."

"You mean we have to get to know and like each other?" asked the young man.

"That's right. As I mentioned earlier, no one likes to deal with people they don't like or with strangers."

"Fine," said the young man thoughtfully. "I can see that no one really likes to negotiate with strangers. But if this relationship is so personal, what can I do to help it develop?"

"The same things you do to develop a relationship with your friends and relatives. You do things that you both like to do. Take a look at yourself. What have you done with your friends lately?"

The young man smiled. "Lots of things. We have dinner parties, I belong to a bowling league, my wife and I play cards with other couples, my next door neighbor and I often go to ball games, and that's just for starters. We're pretty active."

Jackson returned the smile. "It sounds like you have a lot of good ways for fostering relationships. You'll find that developing a Win-Win Relationship is not very different. For example, your friend and mine, the Win-Win Negotiator, is fond of playing golf to get to know other people."

"Fine," said the young man, "but from what you've said, there's more to it than that."

"Right again!" said Jackson. "Part of developing Win-Win Relationships is to cultivate a sense of mutual trust."

Jackson paused for a moment and lifted the telephone receiver from his desk. "With this phone, I can buy and sell millions of dollars worth of products in a matter of minutes. Why? Because the people on the other end of the line trust me. I've never gone back on my word. If I ever did, I'd be all done in the export-import business. You see, my father taught me something very important many years ago. My mother even had it inscribed on the watch they gave me for graduation."

The young man reached across the desk to look at a smoothly worn down watch, bearing an inscription:

***

Your Word Is Your Bond

***

"You've convinced me of the importance of trust in forming Win-Win Relationships," said the young man, "but how do I go about getting people to trust me?"

"Good question," responded Jackson. "It's really not difficult. First of all, it's critical that you not lose sight of the fact that you're trying to develop a sense of trust with another human being. Thus, make sure you go out of your way to be good natured, sociable, accommodating, and polite. In other words, treat the other person the way you would want to be treated."

"I see your point," said the young man.

Jackson continued, "The second thing you need to do is demonstrate the fact that you are honest. You need to show the other person that you have been honest in your dealings with other people."

"Is this where I could mention instances where I have made 'good' on past deals?"

"Right!" said Jackson. "Finally, always make good on your word. Never make promises that you don't intend to keep, and by all means, make sure you keep the promises you make. You see, each 'kept' promise strengthens the bond of trust between you and the other person.''

"Does this mean that the longer the string of promises you have kept with the other person, the higher the level of trust?'' asked the young man.

"It certainly does,'' responded Jackson. "But also keep in mind that even the strongest feeling of trust between you and another person can be undone by only one promise that you fail to keep.''

"It's amazing,'' said the young man, "to think that a sense of trust that may have taken years to develop can be undone so easily.''

"Now you know why 'YOUR WORD IS YOUR BOND' is inscribed on my watch,'' smiled Jackson.

"You've certainly made your point about the importance of trust,'' responded the young man. "Does developing Win-Win Relationships involve anything else?''

"Yes, there is one more thing to keep in mind,'' said Jackson. "Make sure you don't discuss business in earnest until you're sure your relationship with the other party has had a chance to fully develop.''

"What will happen if I do?'' asked the young man.

"Either you'll have a difficult time reaching an agreement or you won't reach an agreement at all. Just as an example, I can see by your ring that you are a married man. Did you ask your wife to marry you on your first date?"

"Of course not. We dated for nearly two years before we got married," said the young man.

"Did you first develop a Win-Win Relationship before you got married?" asked Jackson.

"By what you've described, I think we did. We started our relationship by doing things that we both liked to do, like going out to dinner, going to movies, walking in the park, and sometimes just talking about what we heard in the news or how we spent our day. Sometimes we did things with other friends.

"Now that I think of it, we developed a sense of trust as time went along by being sensitive to each other's needs, sending each other cards, buying each other gifts. I was always buying her flowers. It just seemed like the thing to do."

"But what would have happened if you had 'popped the question' a little too soon?" interjected Jackson.

"I might have blown it," said the young man. "Popping the question too soon could have scared her off, and we may never have gotten married."

"I rest my case," said Jackson.

"I'm impressed with what you're telling me," replied the young man. "But how did you learn about Win-Win Relationships?"

Jackson responded, "Back when I was a salesman, I tried to 'hard-sell' a proposal to a potential customer I had never dealt with before."

"What happened?" asked the young man. "Did he throw you out of his office?"

"No, but he should have, as rude as I was. Instead, this individual took me aside and told me how he appreciated my enthusiasm as a salesman. He then proceeded to tell me essentially what I've told you concerning the importance of building a relationship before discussing business in earnest. Afterwards, he invited me to lunch."

"Did you ever land the account?" asked the young man.

"I certainly did," responded Jackson, "but not until I developed a Win-Win Relationship with this person. Furthermore, I still do a large amount of business with this person today.''

"That person you dealt with seems like one very squared away businessman,'' replied the young man.

"Of course!'' replied Jackson with a smile. "He's the Win-Win Negotiator.''

The two men continued to talk further about developing Win-Win Relationships, but the third step was reserved for another person to describe. As Jackson reviewed the young man's list of Win-Win Negotiators, he selected one who he thought was just the right person and called ahead to introduce the young man.

When the young man returned to his car, he made another entry in his notebook. . . .

Developing a Win-Win Relationship is easy. You need only to:

1. Plan activities which allow a positive personal relationship to develop.

2. Cultivate a sense of mutual trust.

3. Allow the relationship to fully develop before discussing business in earnest.

were accomplished but paid little or no attention to
the other party's goals. Very often, I came away

THE young man's third encounter was with Mr. Larry Alamos, a well dressed man in his early fifties.

"What can I do for you?" he began.

The young man began by describing his meetings with Friedman and Jackson, and what he had learned about Win-Win Plans and Win-Win Relationships. "I'm very anxious to learn about the next step," he said.

"I can see that you are," replied Alamos. After a reflective pause, he continued, "For years I used to pride myself in being one of the toughest and meanest negotiators around. I thought I knew every trick in the book! I used to think that winning a negotiation meant tricking or badgering the other party into agreements that were to my advantage and to his disadvantage. In other words, I made sure my goals were accomplished but paid little or no attention to the other party's goals. Very often, I came away from these negotiations having reached some very favorable agreements. The problem is, however, that these were good deals only on paper that often didn't materialize."

Alamos went on, "You see, if the other party feels he's come out on the short end of the agreement, he has little or no incentive to perform. And why should he? It would often be to his disadvantage if he did. Thus, even though it looked initially like I had won these negotiations, in the end I often lost because the other party chose not to perform adequately."

After another pause, Alamos continued, "It wasn't until I met the Win-Win Negotiator that I learned about forming Win-Win Agreements."

"Win-Win Agreements?" asked the young man.

"Yes," replied Alamos, "That's the next step in the Win-Win Negotiation process."

"But how do Win-Win Agreements differ from any other kind of agreement?" asked the young man.

"In true Win-Win Agreements, the goals of both parties are reconciled into a mutually acceptable agreement. Because of this, both parties have a stake in the agreement and therefore come away committed to holding up their respective ends of it. If there is one thing I've learned, it's this." He handed the young man a plaque from his desk. The plaque read:

***

Agreements Can't Perform Only People Can

***

"What you're saying is that reaching a satisfactory agreement really isn't the ultimate goal of a negotiation, but obtaining satisfactory performance is," interjected the young man.

"Right on!" exclaimed Alamos. "You see, any agreement, no matter how favorable it reads, is worthless if the other party chooses not to honor it."

"Can't I sue for non-performance?" asked the young man.

"Of course," said Alamos, "but a law suit could take years to settle, and still not get what you want from the other party at the time you want it."

"Fascinating," said the young man. "But how do you form a Win-Win Agreement?"

"By putting your Win-Win Plan to work," answered Alamos. "If you've done everything correctly up until now, forming a Win-Win Agreement is not all that difficult."

After a brief pause, Alamos continued, "Let's assume that you have developed a Win-Win Plan and formed a Win-Win Relationship. How would you begin to form a Win-Win Agreement?"

"Well, since my Win-Win Plan would be based on my assumptions about which goals the other party was trying to accomplish, the first thing I'd do would be to confirm the goals of the other party."

"That's correct," said Alamos. "Even the best of plans can fail if they're based on the wrong set of assumptions."

"But how do you confirm the goals of the other party?" asked the young man.

"Simply by asking questions about his goals and listening carefully to the answers," replied Alamos.

"That makes sense," said the young man, "but how do I know I'll get honest answers?"

"If you have taken the time to fully develop a Win-Win Relationship, you have left the other party with no reason to be dishonest or evasive in his answers," responded Alamos.

"I see now why it's so important to develop a Win-Win Relationship before trying to form an agreement," said the young man. "But what if I suspect that some of the other party's answers *are* untrue or evasive?" asked the young man.

"That simply means that you haven't yet developed a Win-Win Relationship with the other party," answered Alamos. "If so, you'll need to spend more time on Step Two of the Win-Win Negotiation process if you expect to reach a Win-Win Agreement."

Alamos continued, "What do you suppose needs to be done next to get a Win-Win Agreement?"

"Let's see," said the young man. "I've confirmed the goals of the other party. Now I guess I'd like to compare those to my own goals and see how far apart we are."

"Or maybe how close you are!" added Alamos.

"That's a positive way of putting it!" responded the young man.

"And why would you do that?" asked Alamos.

"So we don't waste a lot of time hashing over areas where we already agree," answered the young man. "Our valuable time can be better spent resolving those areas where we initially disagree."

"How would you go about verifying those areas of probable agreement?" asked Alamos.

"By stating up front what I thought those areas were and asking the other party to either confirm, deny, or modify my assessment," answered the young man.

"What makes you think the other guy will give you honest answers?" asked Alamos with a smile.

"As you told me earlier," the young man answered, "if I've fully developed a Win-Win Relationship with the other party, he has no reason to be dishonest with me."

"Now, once you've verified those areas where you and the other party already agree, what do you think should come next?" asked Alamos.

"I suppose," said the young man, "it's time to implement one of the Win-Win solutions that I developed as part of my Win-Win Plan."

"Right," said Alamos. "You really are a bright young man. Next, you'd propose the Win-Win solution that you think the other party is most likely to accept. And, it doesn't hurt to do a little selling here, but be careful that you don't come across like you are trying to jam your proposal down the other party's throat. This move would suggest that you think more of your proposal than you do of him, which can deal a serious setback to your relationship. Also keep in mind that the other party probably has a solution that he would also like to propose. If so, make sure he has the same opportunity to sell his proposal as you had to sell yours."

Alamos continued, "After both parties have proposed their solutions, they will most likely find some areas where their proposals agree on how to reconcile existing differences in a Win-Win fashion. These areas of agreement should be acknowledged by both parties since they no longer need to be reconciled."

"What happens to those areas where both parties still disagree?" asked the young man.

"Good question," replied Alamos. "You work to resolve these remaining differences through creative problem solving, brainstorming, and building on each other's ideas. This is the fun part of the Win-Win Negotiation process."

"How does it usually work?" asked the young man.

"Let me give you an example," responded Alamos. "A reputable European manufacturer of paper machinery was attempting to sell its products to a leading paper manufacturer in North America. As it turned out, both firms did a good job of Win-Win Planning and Win-Win Relationship Development. After confirming the buyer's goals and verifying what the two parties already agreed on, the seller proposed a Win-Win solution which reconciled most of the areas where the two parties initially disagreed. After some initial joint problem solving, all areas of disagreement but one were reconciled. The fate of the negotiation finally rested on one last issue."

"What was that?" asked the young man.

"Price," replied Alamos. "The seller wanted to receive a price of about $9 million, but the buyer had a budget of only $7 million. At this point, the situation began to look hopeless, and both parties were starting to get a little edgy.

"So what do you suppose they did?" asked Alamos. "Shake hands and part company? After all, they both had alternative places to do business."

"No!" replied the young man. "If they were Win-Win negotiators, they would never have given up that easily especially if they were that close to an agreement."

"Exactly," said Alamos. "But they started by going back and reviewing all the things they had agreed on — their common ground. This showed them how much they both had to lose if they failed to reach an agreement.''

"I can see where emphasizing common ground would keep both parties thinking Win-Win," interjected the young man, "but how did they ever manage to close the gap on the $2 million in purchase price?''

"Joint problem solving to the rescue," said Alamos. "In this case, both parties again reviewed each other's goals. The buyer wanted to save money, and the seller wanted to make a profit selling his equipment. Consequently, the seller had to have something of equal value in return if he were to give up $2 million in the sale price. At this point, the buyer suggested some used equipment that might be traded, and the seller threw out the idea of extending the payment terms.''

"Both of them worked toward a solution to the problem. I'll bet that helped them reach a Win-Win Agreement," commented the young man.

"It certainly did," said Alamos. "What finally happened is that the seller brought up one of his goals that he hadn't bothered to discuss earlier — to open up the North American Market. As it turned out,

although his firm was very successful in Western
Europe, it had yet to sell its first machine in North
America. When this information hit the table, the
solution seemed to occur to both parties at once: The
buyer proposed that he would help the seller to
showcase his product to the North American market
if the seller would agree to sell the machine for $7
million."

"How did the seller react?" asked the young man.

"Well," answered Alamos, "the seller did some
checking with the home office concerning the size of
the budget for opening the North American market.
He found his company was more than able to sell the
machine for $7 million in exchange for some help in
'showcasing' the product to other paper companies.
With this kind of help, it appeared his company
could be firmly entrenched in the North American
market far ahead of its current projections."

"What happened?" asked the young man.

"Things went just as the seller had figured,"
answered Alamos. "With the help of the paper
company, the European firm did become entrenched

in the North American market far ahead of
schedule.''

"What about the paper company?'' asked the
young man.

Alamos smiled, "They found that the seller
showing an occasional customer through the plant
caused very little inconvenience. In fact, the technical
support that they received from the seller to keep the
'showcase' machine running at peak performance at
all times was another benefit they hadn't even
thought about.''

"So now I ask you, who won the negotiation?''

"No doubt about it,'' replied the young man.
"They both won.''

"Right!'' replied the older man. "But if they
hadn't been thinking of Win-Win, then chances are
they both would have lost. The seller would have
spent a lot more money to try to break into the North
American market, and the buyer might have gone to
a domestic firm and probably still ended up paying
more than $7 million.''

"Fine,'' said the young man, "but may I ask you
one more question?''

"Of course," replied Alamos.

The young man continued, "Let's assume that both parties have gone through the steps of the Win-Win Negotiation process that we've discussed so far. When do they finally reach an agreement?"

"After all of the problems are solved and both sets of goals are reconciled, that *is* the agreement," came the reply. "All you then have to do is write down what you've agreed on."

This time the young man paused for a much longer period. "I think I've got it!" he proclaimed. "I think I know how to form a Win-Win Agreement. But this is only three steps. What's the purpose of the fourth step of the Win-Win Negotiation process?"

As he had come to expect, Alamos did not answer his question. "Let me set you up with an appointment with Ms. Karen McRay. She's the person who represented the paper company in the negotiation I just told you about."

"That would be interesting," said the young man. "Thank you. But just out of curiosity, who represented the European company in that negotiation?"

"I did," replied Alamos with a smile. "I've since moved on to this position, but I've always kept in touch with Ms. McRay. You'll see why when you meet her."

As the young man left Mr. Alamos' office, he began to formulate the next entry for his notebook....

Forming Win-Win Agreements is easy. You need only to:

1.   Confirm the other party's goals.

2.   Verify areas of agreement.

3.   Propose and consider Win-Win solutions to reconcile areas of disagreement.

4.   Jointly resolve any remaining differences.

AFTER lunch, the young man drove across the city to a modern high-rise office building where Ms. McRay's office was located. Ms. McRay turned out to be a very distinguished woman in her mid 50s. Again, the young man was impressed by his warm reception.

"So you want to become a Win-Win Negotiator?" Ms. McRay asked with a smile.

"I sure do," answered the young man enthusiastically. "And based on the good things I've heard about you, I'm at the right place to learn."

"Well, good. I'll do what I can," she replied. "Tell me what you have learned thus far?"

The young man explained what he had been taught about Win-Win Plans, developing Win-Win Relationships, and forming Win-Win Agreements.

"It sounds to me like you're ready for the fourth and final step in the Win-Win Negotiation Process," commented Ms. McRay.

"I guess I am," replied the young man, "but at this point I must admit that I'm puzzled."

"What seems to be troubling you?" asked Ms. McRay.

The young man continued, "I guess I don't see why there has to be a fourth step. If you've done the first three steps correctly, you've already formed a Win-Win Agreement in which both parties are committed to perform. Isn't that what you set out to accomplish in the first place?"

"Not really," replied Ms. McRay. "Remember, we're talking about Win-Win Negotiating, and the end result of Win-Win Negotiating is not just forming a Win-Win Agreement; it's obtaining performance of that agreement! Your assessment would be correct if agreements automatically transformed into performance, but they don't. That's why Win-Win Negotiation has a fourth step. We call it Win-Win Maintenance."

"What you're saying," said the young man, "is that once a Win-Win Agreement has been formed, the next step is to ensure the other party holds up his end of the agreement."

"Right," said Ms. McRay. "That's the Commitment Maintenance aspect of Win-Win Maintenance. There is also a Relationship Maintenance aspect which I'll tell you about shortly."

Ms. McRay continued, "Probably the most fre-
quent mistake that negotiators make is they assume
that once a satisfactory agreement is reached, the
negotiation is finished and satisfactory performance
will be forthcoming. As such, they lose sight of the
fact that it's not the agreement that performs, it's the
people. You see, an agreement, no matter how iron-
clad, cannot guarantee performance. People cannot
be forced to do things against their will. I find it
helpful to think of agreements as pedestrian cross-
walks."

"Pedestrian cross-walks?" questioned the young
man.

"Yes, the kind you find at street intersections in
states like California that are usually marked with
white lines," answered Ms. McRay. "What happens
when you step onto one of these cross-walks?"

"In California, the motorists bring their cars to a
stop until I have crossed the intersection," answered
the young man.

"And why do they stop?" asked Ms. McRay.

"They have to," answered the young man. "It's
the law."

"Have you ever seen anyone break this law?" asked Ms. McRay.

"Many times," answered the young man. "In fact, I have had several close calls myself."

"That's my point," said Ms. McRay. "Even the law cannot guarantee performance because laws, like agreements, can't perform, only people can. That's why I keep this sign in front of me on my desk."

***

*People + Commitment
= Performance*

***

"It serves as a constant reminder that once I have formed a Win-Win Agreement, my job becomes one of keeping the other party committed to holding up their end."

"This explains why many agreements fail to materialize," said the young man. "For one reason or another, people lose their original commitment to an agreement and take their energies elsewhere."

"Exactly!" proclaimed Ms. McRay. "I think you're beginning to understand why the Win-Win method of negotiating has a fourth step."

"I sure am," replied the young man. "But is performing Commitment Maintenance a difficult process?"

"Not really," answered Ms. McRay. "You only need to do two things. First, you need to provide timely and meaningful feedback to the other party based on their holding up their part of the agreement. It's no secret. Feedback based on performance is the number one motivator of people. People committed to results stay committed when they know how they're doing and when they feel their efforts are genuinely appreciated. This is especially true if their performance required some extraordinary effort."

Ms. McRay continued, "Feedback can take many forms. For example, it can take the form of a personal visit to recognize the other party and thank him for his efforts. It can also take the form of a phone call or handwritten note. What's important is that it's timely and it's tied to performance. For example, how do you feel when your boss or someone else important in your life recognizes you for a job well done and goes out of his way to thank you for it?"

"I feel great," said the young man.

"This is why providing feedback based on performance is such an important part of Commitment Maintenance," said Ms. McRay. "People simply like to feel great."

Ms. McRay continued, "The second aspect of Commitment Maintenance is for you to make sure you hold up your end of the agreement. Nothing will diminish the other party's commitment to an agreement faster than you not holding up your end. Remember, we're talking Win-Win Negotiations here which means if you don't hold up your end of a Win-Win Agreement, then the other party can't accomplish his goals. In other words, if he sees holding up his end of the agreement fails to result in the accomplishment of his goals, then what motivation does he have to perform?''

"Not very much," replied the young man.

"That's right," said Ms. McRay. "It's a simple rule. If you don't perform, they won't either."

"Well," said the young man, "you've convinced me of the merits of Commitment Maintenance, but you said there was another aspect of Win-Win Maintenance."

"Right again," replied Ms. McRay. "It's called Relationship Maintenance, and like its name implies, it deals with maintaining the Win-Win Relationship that you have already developed with the other party. The problem with relationships is that if you don't maintain them, they deteriorate. Furthermore, if you let them deteriorate too long, you have to develop them all over before you can effectively deal with the other party again."

"What you're saying," said the young man, "is that if I ever expect to negotiate with a particular person again, it would be wise for me to keep the relationship alive — like you and Mr. Alamos."

"No question about it," replied Ms. McRay. "You see, relationships are a lot like automobiles. They are a lot less trouble to maintain than they are to repair."

"That's like staying in good physical shape," replied the young man. "It's a lot less effort to stay in shape than it is to get there in the first place."

"That's it exactly," responded Ms. McRay with a smile. "I must admit, you do learn fast."

The young man smiled back and said, "I think I understand the importance of maintaining a Win-Win Relationship, but I have one final question."

"Fire away," said Ms. McRay.

The young man continued, "Do I do anything different to maintain a Win-Win Relationship than I did to develop it in the first place?"

"Not at all," replied Ms. McRay. "Just continue doing the same things such as going to lunch or playing golf."

"How often will I need to interact with the other party to maintain a relationship with him?" asked the young man.

"That depends on the other party," responded Ms. McRay. "As we discussed earlier, it will take far fewer encounters with the other party to maintain a Win-Win Relationship than it did to develop it! The key in Relationship Maintenance, however, is to interact with the other party often enough to prevent the relationship from deteriorating.''

"I now have all four steps to the Win-Win Negotiation process,'' remarked the young man. "I can't wait to tell the Win-Win Negotiator all that I have learned. Thank you so much for sharing your time with me.''

"Believe me, the pleasure was all mine,'' Ms. McRay responded with a smile as she walked the young man to the door.

"By the way, do you happen to know the Win-Win Negotiator very well?'' asked the young man as he stopped to shake Ms. McRay's hand.

"I certainly do,'' she replied. "As a matter of fact, we just had lunch together yesterday.''

"I should have figured as much,'' said the young man with a smile.

"I'll call and tell him you're on your way,'' she said smiling back at the young man.

When the young man returned to his car, he took a moment to record in his trusty notebook what he had just learned....

Performing Win-Win Maintenance is simple. You need only to:

1. Maintain Commitment by:
   a. Providing meaningful feedback based on performance.
   b. Holding up your end of the agreement.
2. Maintain the Relationship by:
   a. Keeping in contact.
   b. Reaffirming trust.

As he drove to the Win-Win Negotiator's office, the young man thought about the simplicity of the Win-Win method of negotiation. Each of the four steps made sense — Win-Win Plans, Win-Win Relationships, Win-Win Agreements, and Win-Win Maintenance. "But," he wondered, "why does this method consistently work while the other methods I have learned about often fail? I'll bet the Win-Win Negotiator has the answer."

When the young man arrived at the Win-Win Negotiator's office, the secretary once again greeted him warmly and said, "Go right in. Ms. McRay called to say you were on your way, so he's expecting you."

"I understand you've been doing some visiting," said the Win-Win Negotiator motioning the young man back to the same comfortable chair he had occupied before.

"I sure have," said the young man enthusiastically, "and have I learned a lot!"

"Well, tell me all about it," said the Win-Win Negotiator, settling in to enjoy the tales.

"I found out why you call yourself the Win-Win Negotiator," he began. "You develop Win-Win

Plans that take into account both your goals and the goals of the people you're negotiating with as well.

"You then develop Win-Win Relationships whereby you and the people you're dealing with feel good about each other and can therefore deal with each other comfortably.

"You form Win-Win Agreements where both parties accomplish their goals and therefore have a strong incentive to live up to their end of the agreement.

"Finally, you engage in Win-Win Maintenance whereby you provide positive feedback which not only encourages people to honor their commitments, but maintains the Win-Win Relationships as well."

"Well, what do you think about this method of negotiating?" asked the Win-Win Negotiator.

"I can't believe how simple and easy it is!" exclaimed the young man. "Yet it seems to work. It results in agreements which are not only favorable, but agreements which also last."

"You have learned a lot, but you must have some questions," said the Win-Win Negotiator.

"Well," said the young man, "I know Win-Win Negotiating works well for you and your friends, but will it work well for me, too?''

"Of course it will!" insisted the Win-Win Negotiator. "That is, if you're willing to do it."

"Maybe so," said the young man, "but I guess I'd be more inclined to use your method if I understood a little more about *why* it works."

"I can appreciate that," said the Win-Win Negotiator. "It's difficult, at best, to put a lot of faith in a method of doing things if you don't understand why it works. Let's start by looking at how the method's four steps fit together."

The Win-Win Negotiator then took out a legal pad and drew what appeared to be a large donut with WIN-WIN written in the middle. The Win-Win Negotiator then divided the donut into four equal sections and then wrote a key word in each of its sections, tore off the sheet of paper, and handed it to the young man. It read:

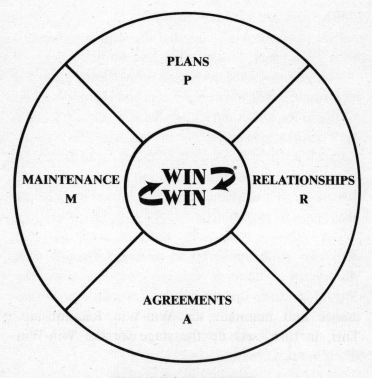

THE PRAM MODEL:
THE WIN-WIN NEGOTIATION PROCESS

"I call this my PRAM model, which is an acronym for Plans, Relationships, Agreements and Maintenance," said the Win-Win Negotiator. "What do you see when you look at it?" he asked the young man.

"I see a circle," said the young man.

"Exactly," said the Win-Win Negotiator. "And what does a circle normally symbolize?"

"Continuity?" said the young man with a puzzled look on his face.

"That's it," replied the Win-Win Negotiator. "And continuity means that something doesn't end. Win-Win negotiating is a continuous process. As the diagram shows, it begins with the development of a Win-Win Plan. This Plan, in turn, requires a Win-Win Relationship if it's going to result in a Win-Win Agreement. The Win-Win Agreement then requires Win-Win Maintenance in order to ensure performance and maintain the Win-Win Relationship. This, in turn, sets up the stage for the Win-Win Planning step the next time around."

"Are you saying that with people you negotiate with on a recurring basis that the process is never over?" asked the young man.

"Precisely," said the Win-Win Negotiator. "Probably the biggest mistake most negotiators make is that they approach each negotiation as if it were a singular event instead of a continuous process. For whatever the reason, these people believe that a negotiation starts when they make eye contact with the person they are going to negotiate with and ends when they shake hands after they've reached an agreement."

"Do you mean," asked the young man, "that most negotiators concentrate the bulk of their efforts on the Agreement Formation step of the process and spend relatively little effort on the Planning, Relationship Development, and Maintenance steps?"

"Exactly!" said the Win-Win Negotiator emphatically. "Most people don't realize there are four necessary steps to the negotiation process. As a result, they can't realize that each prior step in the process must be done properly if the next step is to have a chance of being successful. Furthermore, since they don't understand that the negotiation process is continuous, they don't realize that their conduct after the agreement is reached determines the level of performance they receive and lays the groundwork for the planning step the next time around.''

"Wow," said the young man. "If you consider this information and combine it with the fact that most people approach a negotiation with the attitude of trying to beat their opponent, there is little wonder why those other negotiating methods I've tried produced such poor results.''

"Right on," said the Win-Win Negotiator. "Any more questions?''

"Just one more," answered the young man.

"Yes?" smiled the Win-Win Negotiator.

"Do all negotiations lend themselves to Win-Win outcomes?''

"Good question," replied the Win-Win Negotiator. "I can't say with 100% certainty that they all do, but I haven't come across a situation yet that didn't have a Win-Win solution hiding in it somewhere. I will have to admit, however, that it takes a lot longer to find a Win-Win solution in some situations than in others. Let me give you an example of a negotiation where all the parties involved were convinced that an acceptable settlement could not be reached.''

"Is this the incident the feature story in the evening paper was written about?'' asked the young man.

The Win-Win Negotiator smiled proudly as he began to unravel the story. . . .

"ACTUALLY, the story began many years ago. In fact, this is where I met Karen McRay. The situation involved a school teachers' association in a nearby town which was trying to come to terms on a three year contract package with the school board. The present contract had 18 months before it expired and already the two parties were miles apart on a number of issues.

"I became involved because the chairman of the school board was a personal friend. The day he called me, he was crying the blues about how bad his situation was. He said cynically, 'Your Win-Win method of negotiating might work in theory, but it certainly doesn't hold up in the real world. I'll bet even you couldn't find a Win-Win solution to this mess.'

"I think he intended his little challenge to be taken tongue-in-cheek, for he seemed quite surprised when I said, 'I'll bet I can. Let's have lunch tomorrow and talk about it.'

"'Fine,' the board chairman agreed, 'but this time I think you've bitten off more than you can chew.'

"The next day at lunch, the first thing I did was to take out a piece of paper and draw the four step PRAM model of the Win-Win Negotiation process — much the same as I did with you. I then explained what the Win-Win Negotiation process is, what each of the steps involves and why each is necessary.

"As he was looking at the four step model, I asked the board chairman what the first step in the Win-Win Negotiation process was.

"'Develop a Win-Win Plan,' he responded.

"'All right,' I said, 'and what do we need to do to develop a Win-Win Plan?'

"'Determine the goals for each of the parties involved in the negotiations and then figure out how to reconcile those goals,' he replied.

"'Now we're getting somewhere,' I told him. 'We can start by asking each group to describe its goals. But, politics and personalities being what they are, we may have to ask several times before we get the real answers.'

"I told the board chairman that I would be happy to serve as fact finder and meet with both groups. I further suggested that we start by determining the goals of the school board since that group was the easiest to approach.

"Several weeks later, the chairman convened a special, closed-door session of the school board to discuss its goals. When I initially broached the subject, I got some pretty nasty remarks. For example, one board member said he wanted to 'see those teachers put in their place,' while another said she wanted to 'fire the whole bunch and start over.'

"I gave them some time to blow off steam before asking them if those goals closely resembled the responsibilities they were elected to fulfill. It didn't take too long for my message to sink in and soon we were outlining some more honorable goals like:

1. Keep teachers' salaries and benefits within budgeted levels.
2. Provide for a quality education.
3. Develop a school system that they could be proud of.

"A month later, I set up a meeting with the teachers' association to determine its goals. At first they responded with 'knee jerk' reactions like the school board's initial comments, but then the group settled down to laying out some realistic goals:

1. Obtaining a five percent pay raise for each of the next three years.
2. Having smaller class sizes and more money appropriated for teachers' aides.
3. Making their school system one of the best in the state.

"During our next luncheon, I showed the board chairman the goals from each group and how they had a common interest in making the school system one of the best.

" 'Well, at least they seem to agree on something,' he said, 'but what's your Win-Win Negotiation Plan to reconcile all of these other goals?'

" 'Glad you asked,' I said. 'I think these goals can best be reconciled if we put together a small committee composed of three members of each group. If we try to put everyone in a room and hash it out, nothing will get accomplished. A small group is a lot less likely to get frustrated and drift back to name calling. This committee can then hammer out an agreement that they all can live with, that is, a Win-Win Agreement.'

" 'They'll kill each other!' shouted the board chairman. 'The teachers and the board members have been at each other's throats for months now. How can you expect them to sit down beside each other and peacefully work out an agreement?'

" 'If we ask them to hammer out an agreement right now, you're absolutely right,' I told the board chairman. 'That's why developing Win-Win Relationships and not formulating Win-Win Agreements is the second step in the Win-Win Negotiation process. You see, these people don't even know each other. For example, if you take any given community, teachers tend to socialize with other teachers and not so much with the rest of the community. They do this because these are the people they have the most in common with. As a result, the board, as well as the rest of the community, really doesn't know the school teachers very well and vice versa. That's why there is so much 'we versus they' or 'them versus us' talk today. It's easy to go for the throat or otherwise insult someone you don't know, but it's pretty hard to do that to someone you've grown to like and appreciate as a human being.'

"'I see your point,' said the board chairman, 'but how do we go about building relationships between these groups?'

"'We have to get them together in a non-business setting,' I suggested. 'I'd be happy to host a cocktail party at the country club, if it's okay with you.'

"'Sounds good to me,' said the board chairman. 'And the two of us can make sure that teachers don't just talk to teachers and board members don't just talk to board members,' he added.

"I winked at the board chairman and said, 'I think you're catching on to how Win-Win Negotiation works.'

"Well, the cocktail party was a rousing success. Both groups of people laughed a lot, had a good time and, most importantly, got to know each other as people. In fact, such a good time was had by everyone, that it was suggested that we do it again. So three months later we had an evening potluck picnic at the Sportsman's Club. Teachers and board members alike were amazed at how much they had in common. At this point, the process was working and Win-Win Relationships were developing.

"The next step was a bit more involved but crucial to the process. During the next several months, the board chairman and I organized a community picnic designed to strengthen the Win-Win Relationship between the parties and bring the common goal of developing a strong school system in front of the general public as well as the taxpayers. We received a great deal of help from the parent-teacher organization who took it upon themselves to hand out the invitations door to door. The event was designed to be self-supporting, and, because of their efforts and the efforts of some local media personalities, the turnout was great. There were games for the kids and games for the adults. The board chairman and I saw to it that the board members and teachers ended up participating in games, and mingling with the other members of the community. As with the previous event, the people who attended the picnic had so much fun, they wanted to have another in the fall. One of the farmers, who happened to have a huge shed, suggested we hold it at his place.

"As we were having lunch the following Monday, the board chairman asked, 'Where do we go from here?'

"'Since relationships between the parties have developed very well, it's time to move on to the next step of the Win-Win negotiation process,' I answered. 'We now need to pull together the joint committee and let them formulate a Win-Win Agreement.'

"I then convened the first meeting of the task force in my conference room. The group agreed to meet on Wednesday evenings for as long as it took to reach an agreement that they all felt good about.

"I'll have to admit it took over three months before a final agreement was reached, but the process of reaching that agreement was a joy to observe. The discussions were not embroiled with bitterness and resentment, because everyone in the room knew each other as sensitive human beings. They directed their energies toward attacking their mutual problems rather than attacking each other. The only voices that were raised, were raised in excitement as breakthroughs in the discussion occurred.

"In the end, the teachers agreed they would see to it that their students received an education second to none if they could get some additional resources. They would need smaller class sizes in certain subjects to allow the teachers to more thoroughly grade and critique homework and provide individualized feedback to students.

"The school board group supported the teachers' assessment but noted that if the additional personnel were hired to allow for smaller class sizes and more individual attention, then the tax paying community could afford only a three percent raise. It was pointed out that the community was in the middle of a recession and funds were very limited. The board members did unanimously agree, however, that if the teachers could live with three percent now, they would pledge to make up the difference once the recession was over.

"Because such a strong sense of trust between the teachers and the board members had developed, the teachers agreed to accept the three percent raise for now. As a result, everyone came away feeling good. It was truly a Win-Win Agreement.

"Shortly afterwards, the board chairman dropped

into my office and said, 'Well you've certainly made a believer out of me. That Win-Win system of yours really works, even in the real world. I just can't believe all that has happened in the last 18 months. It's truly amazing what people can do when they work together instead of against each other. I guess we've completed the job, haven't we?'

" 'Not so fast,' I cautioned him. 'We're not done yet.'

" 'We're not?' he asked.

"I asked him to pull out the diagram of the Win-Win Negotiation process that I had drawn for him 18 months earlier. He reached into his briefcase and pulled out a rather tattered piece of legal paper with the four step PRAM model on it. 'We haven't gone through all the steps in the Win-Win Negotiation process,' I said.

"He stared at the model for a moment and said, 'I guess we haven't done anything about Win-Win Maintenance, have we?'

" 'No', I said. 'The thing we can't afford to do is let these relationships, that we have worked so hard to build up, fall apart. This means we need to continue to have social events between school teachers and the school board at least several times per year. We also need to have one or more community events where teachers, board members and the rest of the community continue to get to know each other better. Finally, we need to remember to say 'thank you' in a meaningful way to anyone who puts forth an outstanding effort in making any of this possible. Always remember, it's the 'thank you,' on top of the pay check, that motivates people to work above and beyond the call of duty. This includes remembering our promise to the teachers once the recession is over.'

"The board chairman quipped as we shook hands, 'You know, Win-Win negotiating sure does beat screaming and hollering at people. It not only produces better results, but it makes life more fun besides.'"

Very impressed, the young man looked at the Win-Win Negotiator and said, "That is one amazing story. I see now why the article in the paper referred to you as the 'negotiator's negotiator.'"

"Well, that was a number of years ago," said the

Win-Win Negotiator. "Since then, a lot more has happened. For example, the school system is rated as one of the top five in the state. What's more, the Chamber of Commerce has been able to use the reputation of the school system to attract new businesses to our community. This has resulted in lower property taxes and higher property values.

"Also, the community hasn't forgotten its promise to the teachers. Today those teachers are among the best supported in the state. And these are just some of the results. Every year another article like the one you just read comes out detailing new benefits to the community."

"But tell me," said the young man, "how did you happen to meet Ms. McRay in the midst of all this?"

"Oh!" laughed the Win-Win Negotiator, "I nearly forgot. She was the lead negotiator for the teachers' association. We became good friends, and as she worked her way into her present position, our relationship has remained."

"I'm amazed," said the young man. "Everybody really did win."

"There's no need to be amazed," said the Win-Win Negotiator. "It's inevitable. In Win-Win Negotiation, *everybody* wins!"

As the young man was getting ready to leave, the Win-Win Negotiator said, "You know, you are a very bright and energetic young man. I sure hope someone like you applies for the managerial position I have open."

"I already have," said the young man enthusiastically.

"I know," beamed the Win-Win Negotiator as he shook the young man's hand. "Welcome aboard!"

OVER the years the young man became successful in every aspect of his life — his career, his marriage, and his family. The reason he was successful was that he approached everything in his life with four basic steps:

1. **Win-Win Plans**
2. **Win-Win Relationships**
3. **Win-Win Agreements**
4. **Win-Win Maintenance**

Yes, the young man had become a Win-Win Negotiator. He had found and mastered the secret to success.

APPENDIX

A Summary. . .

There are four steps to Win-Win negotiation that almost anyone can perform with ease. These steps include Plans, Relationships, Agreements, and Maintenance.

Establishing Win-Win Plans is simple. You need only to:

1. Agree on your own goals.
2. Anticipate the goals of the other party.
3. Determine areas of probable agreement.
4. Develop Win-Win solutions to reconcile areas of probable disagreement.

Developing a Win-Win Relationship is easy. You need only to:

1. Plan activities which allow a positive personal relationship to develop.
2. Cultivate a sense of mutual trust.
3. Allow the relationship to fully develop before discussing business in earnest.

Forming Win-Win Agreements is easy. You need only to:

1. Confirm the other party's goals.
2. Verify areas of agreement.
3. Propose and consider Win-Win solutions to reconcile areas of disagreement.
4. Jointly resolve any remaining differences.

Performing Win-Win Maintenance is simple. You need only to:

1. Maintain Commitment by:
    a. Providing meaningful feedback based on performance.
    b. Holding up your end of the agreement.
2. Maintain the Relationship by:
    a. Keeping in contact.
    b. Reaffirming trust.

The PRAM Model...

The Win-Win Negotiator approaches all problems with four basic steps. Since Win-Win negotiating is a continuous process, the four steps form a circle:

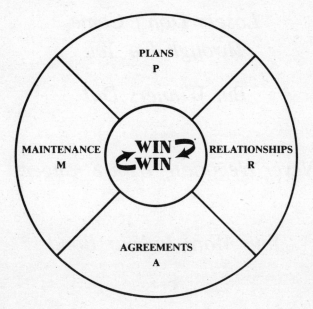

THE WIN-WIN NEGOTIATION PROCESS

Step One — Establishing Win-Win Plans

Step Two — Developing Win-Win Relationships

Step Three — Forming Win-Win Agreements

Step Four — Performing Win-Win Maintenance

Gems Worth Remembering...

***

*Losers Don't Come
Through For You*

But Winners Do!

***

Never Negotiate With Strangers

***

Your Word Is Your Bond

***

*Agreements Can't Perform
Only People Can*

***

*People + Commitment
= Performance*

***